T0197346

THE LAST LAP
SHELDON BRODSKY'S
INSIGHTFUL GUIDE TO
THE JOYS OF RETIREMENT

A "TELL IT LIKE IT IS" ACCOUNT OF ONE MAN'S
RETIREMENT EXPERIENCES DESIGNED TO
MAKE YOU PAUSE AND TAKE A LONG, HARD
LOOK BEFORE YOU LEAP

By

MARTIN C. MAYER

Order this book online at www.trafford.com
or email orders@trafford.com

Most Trafford titles are also available at major online book retailers.

Printed in the United States of America.

ISBN: 978-1-4669-0950-2 (sc)
ISBN: 978-1-4669-0952-6 (hc)
ISBN: 978-1-4669-0951-9 (e)

Library of Congress Control Number: 2011963223

Trafford rev. 04/27/2012

 www.trafford.com

North America & international
toll-free: 1 888 232 4444 (USA & Canada)
phone: 250 383 6864 ♦ fax: 812 355 4082

CHAPTER ONE
THE LAST LAP?

Hello. My name is Sheldon Brodsky, and I am not the typical New York putz who works his tuchas off at some business or profession and then comes to Florida to die.

No siree. I got lucky. Very lucky. I indeed worked my tuchas off for many years as a sole practitioner C.P.A. in the City because, frankly, my defective personality actually enjoyed the grind.

I did not plan to quit or retire, but then I got lucky. A large C.P.A. firm offered me three million dollars for my practice, and I had to make an immediate decision to sell or not to sell.

Three million dollars is a shitload of money. It took me several seconds to make up my mind, and I am ashamed to admit that I hadn't even researched the Federal and New York State income tax ramifications of my decision when I gleefully signed on the dotted line. Possibly, that does not speak well of me as a talented C.P.A., but frankly, I succumbed to some instant gratification need to change the lifestyle I told myself I enjoyed but probably implicitly hated enough to get away from it rapidly and without considering any of the negative ramifications of my decision.

In truth, that is typically the way I have always done things. I admit that I have a major personality defect which I jokingly refer to as "flotsam-jetsam" syndrome.

The "flotsam-jetsam" syndrome is a mutation of a live and let live personality orientation. Because I am kind of a loner, it is difficult for me to relate to others or integrate my own daily comings and goings with those of the people who know me or depend on me. So, I tend to plod onward in the routine which seems to be comfortable while buffering any daily slings and arrows which could possibly deflect me from what I *think* seems comfortable to me.

My problem appears to be that I give a crap about something only when it is convenient to do so, and if giving a crap causes me discomfort or upsets my routine, I kid myself into *believing* that I give a crap when I actually don't. Believing that I do gives me comfort while it excuses me in my own mind from accepting real responsibility of *really* giving a crap.

That probably accounts for why my wife left me without explanation after twenty-six years of marriage and why my two sons of that union, after graduating from Dartmouth and Penn respectively, moved far away to California and Oregon. They must have figured out the disconnect between what I say and what I really do. I told myself that I should probably care about these situations, but to do so would require me to lose focus on the routine of earning a living (and *really* give a crap).

I sincerely doubt that my wife's departure had anything to do with her ongoing affair with her personal trainer. He dumped her summarily after she left.

My two sons still do occasionally contact me. It happens when they need money or are in some other kind of pickle. This usually results in my having to send them a few bucks, but then I would just take on a couple of new clients to make up the outflow of cash.

Possibly now you will be getting some insight into what is wrong with my personality. I know I have a defect of some kind, but knowing I have one and doing something about it are not the same thing. Running away to Florida without really thinking out the equation ahead of time is an example of how I tell myself I give a crap when I am merely kidding myself into believing I really do as a way to avoid *really* giving a crap.

Possibly, that also accounts for why the lawyer who represented me in the divorce is mad as hell at me. I let my wife have anything she wanted, which was just about everything we jointly possessed. He really had no understanding of matrimonial law because his practice was real estate oriented, and this was the first matrimonial matter he had ever handled.

My lump sum settlement generosity I extended to my ex-wife proved to have been a blessing in disguise, (no thanks to my lawyer who advised me against it because he *did* give a crap) because now that wretch can't come after me for any part of my three million dollar bonanza! In the long run, cash is king, and my focus on cash appears to be the center of my existence and the compelling reason I snapped at the offer to sell my practice without reasoning out the consequences to my lifestyle this decision would bring.

Frankly, had I not been offered three million for my practice, I would probably still be the same 5'9", slightly built, 155 lb., 65 year old workaholic. Every morning I would get up at 6AM, gobble down my non-nutritious on-the-fly breakfast, sprint to the train from my Long Island home while juggling my umbrella and briefcase, fidget all the way to Manhattan, and arrive before the clock would strike 9AM.

But now, I have made a hasty exit to the Sunshine State. I sublet my rented condo (the ex got the house), put most of my belongings in storage, and caught the first flight out of JFK airport to West Palm Beach.

Now that I am financially on Easy Street, you might be asking yourself what my motivation could possibly be for writing this guide to Sunbelt retirement. It is based upon two years of dealing with this situation.

Good question. It is not for the money. It is not for any kind of recognition (remember, I told you I am a kind of loner who shies away from personal relationships or deep involvements). It is because I have an irrational need to leave a legacy for those people who believe that South Florida is the equivalent of the Promised Land and who come here with unrealistic expectations as to what this neck of the woods is really about.

So, gird yourself, and read on. I plan to tell it like it *really* is, so in the event you are offered three million dollars to escape the daily grind of wherever you are, you will think long and hard before you make the plunge, unless, of course, all you seek is a warm climate in which to pass your final days.

CHAPTER TWO
THE ACTIVE ADULT COMMUNITY

Shortly after arriving in West Palm Beach, I set about the task of finding a place to live. I had heard that a newcomer should never rush into things but should rent at first, get to know the territory, and then purchase a permanent residence. As you will learn when you read on, I took the overall of this advice with a grain of salt.

What truly surprised me was the proliferation in these parts of Active Adult Communities.

Here in Southern Florida, community leaders have figured out a neat way to attract ratables without placing the expensive burden of schools on their community or regional budgets.

The objective in approving residential developments restricted to occupants 55 years of age or older is to exclude as much as possible residents of child bearing age. Where there are no children in permanent residence there is no need to provide costly schooling facilities.

In their infinite wisdom (or lack thereof) these local legislators often fail to take into account the cost of additional police and fire services, medical emergency services, and other necessary social services offered at taxpayer expense to senior citizens.

Be that as it may, Palm Beach County has received possibly more than its fair share of such retirement or semi-retirement communities with many more in the planning stages.

Prior to the current down cycle in the residential real estate market, developers used to run lotteries to determine who gets first dibs at the privilege of occupying these cloistered enclaves. And prices were often bid up rather than down.

In any event, what has not changed, despite lower pricing, are the many strange restrictions one has to endure in Active Adult communities and in gated communities whether age restricted or not. Prior Constitutional entitlements at our prior residences considered or not, most of these communities host a myriad of rules and restrictions which might even boggle the mind of a Philadelphia lawyer.

For example, the Board of Directors may have the right to restrict the color of your home to a narrow variety of hues which they alone can approve. The Board can determine the frequency of lawn mowing, tree trimming, whether you can erect a garbage shed (and where you can erect it), whether you can park a truck overnight in your driveway, whether any of your vehicles can sport commercial advertising, and whether you can keep your garage door open when you are not physically in your garage.

If that were not enough to abridge Constitutional freedoms, mailboxes may have to look exactly alike, and you may be prohibited from placing your lawn chair on your own front lawn, drinking beer in the front yard, or lounging in front of your own home in an undershirt.

So many of these silly prohibitions are of the *mala prohibita* variety and not mala in se, so you find yourself at the mercy of whichever of your neighbors happens to be serving on the Board at any given time.

That is why, when I first got here, I avoided all the restricted and gated communities and opted for a cute little rental cottage made out of cinder block and which was situated in a pastoral setting on the outskirts of town.

What a relief I thought it would be to avoid all of those silly restrictions, association assessments, and unwanted contact with cookie cutter neighbors living in cookie cutter houses too close to each other for real privacy.

However, my self-congratulations quickly proved to be premature and unwarranted. A few days after I moved in, when the wind blew in an Easterly direction, I detected a horrendous stench emanating from a property some 2,000 feet down the road but lying outside of the incorporated boundary of my community.

Upon exploration, this proved to be a pig farm protected by the zoning codes because it constituted a pre-existing, non-conforming usage.

It was only then that I understood why the crafty broker who leased this place to me had filled the vacant home prior to the showing with roses, lilacs and petunias. It also explained the existence of two empty spray containers of Febreze in the garage.

It is a good thing that I possess accounting background. I quickly calculated the cost of year's worth of Febreze and added same to the cost of my base rent and ancillary upcharges. Then, for two dollars, I purchased a wall calendar to mark off each of the twelve months of my lease as they expired.

So, do not rush into a purchase of a home when you come to Florida. Rent first, and get to know the territory. Better yet, stay in a hotel for a few weeks until you have a good idea as to where you should rent long term rather than ever purchase. Find an honest real estate professional who values a longer term relationship with you rather than turning a fast dollar. I really can't understand how I missed that my broker suffered from the same personality defect I suffer from and placed cash above every other consideration. Shame on him! Shame on *me!*

CHAPTER THREE
TREPIDATION AND RECRIMINATION

I joined a country club. I did this to find tennis partners and pick up on one of the real joys I had when I lived on Long Island. I really did not know precisely what I was to expect on this first day of membership. As I picked up my tennis gear and loaded it into my newly acquired Chevy SUV I felt like I was about to experience the first day of the rest of my life.

For me, it was a self-fulfilling anticlimactic prophecy that retirement should feel like a vacation but should not have a finite ending, as did most vacations taken to escape temporarily the rigors and responsibilities of my successful career as a self employed Certified Public Accountant.

Somehow, I acknowledged that this day had an additional dimension to it. No longer would I look forward to returning to my workplace in the City. That was history. Instead, I would now experience this day of recreation as an end unto *itself* and not a means to an end, as tennis vacations had previously been defined in my psyche—as something to get through so I could return to work.

The trouble I was presently experiencing in evaluating the immediate reality, however, is that it felt like the same kind of anxiety I used to experience on workdays while traveling from my suburban residence to my office in the city. I used to gird myself for tolerating that daily grind by projecting how good it would feel, at the end of the workday, to be on my way home to spend what I perceived to be an enjoyable, relaxing evening with my wife and two sons. In retrospect, the enjoyment must have been mine alone, since she left me, and the boys pretty well ignore my existence.

Now, however, I was struggling to evaluate and put in an affirmative perspective the decision I had made to retire, move to Palm Beach county in Florida, and otherwise live the good life of a man who had paid his dues in the business world, had worked hard for every nickel he possessed, and who was now entitled to savor the sweet fruit of his labors.

If only the flavor of that sweet fruit could be defined in terms of *my own* inbred values instead of some abstract projection of values I believed everybody else had, my state of mind might have lapsed at least into a pragmatic "first experience it and then wait and see" format.

Instead, I was rhetorically asking myself where it had been written that I should retire at age sixty-five, redirect body and soul into channels most of my *peers* believed induced quiet enjoyment, and otherwise alter the focus upon productivity that was etched into my modus operandi by years of primary devotion to business callings and had been the most important essence of my prior existence.

I am loathe to admit that I actually harbored a deep seated resentment of the system which had orchestrated a format of such expectations, so I simply was not able to look forward to a morning of tennis confrontations with a bunch of old players whose skills levels were questionable. This whole thing was sure to be gesture in futility and serve only to consume time and space. Worst of all, it was not a vacation to be tolerated until I could once again return to my familiar workplace and do something really productive.

The reality, indeed, was that I had sold my accounting practice for three million dollars and was now supposed to enjoy the rest of my life spending my earned profit on meaningful non-business endeavors. This was the time in life to enrich my soul and my spirit but not my bank account. For a man who had always lived by the cash is king philosophy, this reality was difficult to swallow.

On some level of consciousness I was forced to acknowledge that I did not have a clear definition of the concept "to live" and did not know where or how to find a level of personal satisfaction which I knew must be implicit in that concept.

Clueless, I observed myself throwing my tennis paraphernalia into the back of my newly acquired SUV and driving off in the direction the country club.

For the present, wait and see and waste and see appeared to be interchangeable concepts.

CHAPTER FOUR
VISITING THE DERMATOLOGIST

Most of the retirees who come to South Florida from the Northeast are seeking refuge from cold weather and snow and relief from the daily grind of earning a livelihood.

Most have no idea as to how to deal with the subtropical sun and the pervasive damage it can do to unprotected skin surfaces. Most have no prior experience with a daily routine of slathering on 30 to 45 sunscreen or the necessity to do so.

Hence, if one didn't migrate to Florida with some pre-existing skin condition, one is almost certain to develop a skin problem, which necessitates a visit or two to the dermatologist's office.

And so it was with me. I had done a painful number on myself the previous day by playing tennis for two hours in the hot sun without the benefit of having coated myself ahead of time with sunscreen lotion.

The dermatologist's waiting room reminded me of my prior experiences in the Army. The Doctor's receptionist had instructed me when I called for the appointment to arrive fifteen minutes ahead of time in order to fill out patient information and insurance forms.

When I arrived at the Doctor's office I went to the receptionist's desk and logged in my arrival time and time of appointment. I could not help but notice that four other patients who had signed in immediately before me were scheduled for the same doctor and at the same appointment time as my own. This was the classic "hurry up and wait" methodology practiced by the U.S. Army, and I was sure that my appointment for this simple problem was now going to keep me at the dermatologist's office for at least two hours. After all, retired seniors really didn't have much of a life, and it was no big deal to make them wait around for medical services. Further, since insurance was paying the bill for the visit, it wasn't the insurance carrier who would be inconvenienced by any delay in rendering services.

So, off to the magazine rack I went to while away the time until I would be reached. The magazine rack contained issues of People, Time, U.S. News and World Report and similar popular magazines.

I could not help but notice that the most recent issue of any of the magazines was at least six months old. I was certain that the Doctor had not invested in any subscriptions but was purchasing his magazines second hand from a nearby thrift shop.

When I was finally reached on the appointment schedule, some hour and 15 minutes beyond the appointed time, a nurse ushered me into an examination room and told me to remove all of my clothes.

I protested, asserting that I had come here only to have treatment for the severe sunburn on my arms and legs. The nurse replied that all new patients must undergo a mandatory full body skin examination so that a record could be made of all growths, warts, freckles and any other aberration on any skin surface. For whose benefit? I found myself rhetorically asking. I had not come here to get the wart on my crotch removed. I had come to live with that wart over the years!

Suddenly, I had a flashback of last month's visit to the podiatrist, at which visit the Doctor's assistant took a complete set of six foot x-rays, gave me a whirlpool footbath treatment and clipped my toenails, all as a prerequisite to permitting me to confer with the Doctor over the fungus condition on my left big toenail!

This is just another obvious Medicare rip-off, I thought, as I hastily redressed myself before the Doctor arrived. I then made a beeline exit from the premises.

In retrospect, I was sure that I might have spared myself the entire happenstance had I simply purchased one of the over the counter sunburn relief medicines from my local pharmacist. But that might have deprived the clerks at Medicare their job of processing claims, and I would otherwise not have had to pay for the skin crème, which, as a generic prescription, was totally covered by my medical insurance.

However, saving the cost of the sunburn ointment was definitely not worth the hassle and humiliation of having the wart on my crotch leered at by the Doctor's nurse, and possibly having been talked into getting it removed.

So, on the way home I stopped at the drug store and purchased a large bottle of over the counter sunburn lotion. I admit that this act was anathema to my cash is king philosophy. Medicare should have had to pay for this remedy.

As I generously rubbed the nonprescription goose grease on my sunburned limbs, in the privacy of own home, I rhetorically validated my decision that it is better to be right than to be the President!

CHAPTER FIVE
THE EARLY BIRD SPECIAL

Anyone who has had any experience in the restaurant business knows that managing payroll, overhead and product wastage are the key factors in turning a profit.

Most retires, including affluent ones, are extremely cost conscious because they harbor an unspoken fear of running out of money prior to their lives running out. The phenomenon has little to do with their pre-retirement standard of living but more to do with the realization that income in senior years is usually less than what was earned when fully employed, even where retirement funds have been prudently invested in income producing passive undertakings.

Hence, in areas where retirees congregate in unusually large numbers, we see the phenomenon of the Early Bird Special. An honestly executed Early Bird Special never reduces either the quality or quantity of the food offered on its menu but only the traditional posted pricing if taken advantage of during Early Bird Special hours.

The challenge for restaurant entrepreneurs is to make a profit on these prices reduced specials while leaving the patron convinced that he has received a bargain for his money. Some restaurateurs accomplish this by overcharging for the same specialties on their regular menu while posting the equitable price for the same dish on the Early Bird Special menu, thus creating a perception in the mind of the Early Bird diner that by dining during a downtime hour at his favorite restaurant he is being rewarded for the relatively small sacrifice of being required to eat dinner at tea time instead of at dinner time.

Other more honorable restaurant operators factor in operating realities that they pay the same rent for their premises during off hours, keep key people on the payroll during off hours, and actually reduce wastage by hyphenating the Early Bird Menu with a smaller selection of main dishes than appear on the full list price menu. So, even if a smaller profit is realized on an Early Bird diner, the patronage still turns out to be profitable and might otherwise not have been experienced at all at the full list price at regular dinner hours.

The same business philosophy can be and sometimes is applied to prices for alcoholic beverages, the item on most menus that carries the largest gross profit spread of any other menu offering. It does not take great scholarship to figure out that four glasses of wine at $5.00 per glass, as opposed to the regular price of $7.50 per glass still earn a decent gross profit to the restaurant when doled out of a $7.00 bottle of wine.

It took me only a few months of full time Florida residency to zero in, by trial and error, on my favorite restaurants, and I quickly realized that a cadre of my new found "friends" and acquaintances at the country club espoused the same philosophy of eating at tea time and falling into the "Boca Midnight" tradition of retiring early at 10:00.

So, after listening to the opinions of others as to the quality rankings of the local bistros, I gave the Early Bird Special at one of the more popular restaurants a try. Then, I did it again at another. Then, I did again at another. Then, I did it again at another.

After that, I never did it again because I simply could not deal with the fact that all of the patrons were old, the serving help was not as polite to Early Birds as they are to the later, full list price diners, and I could not get over the feeling in my gut that I was stealing something from the proprietor who was letting me get away with it simply because I am a senior citizen.

Further, I could not deal with a parking lot full of Toyotas and Nissans because I have always resented the way the Japanese have stolen the American auto industry out from under us!

CHAPTER SIX
QUIET IN THE THEATER

It has been said in many quarters that the most rude and inconsiderate audiences in the entire United States can be found in Florida, and most particularly, in southeastern Florida.

There is probably a logical explanation for this phenomenon, but one can only speculate that it has something to do with the average age of the audiences and their sense of entitlement.

It is not that the elderly people who frequent the stage and movie performances do not understand that being quiet during the performance is just plain the courteous thing to do. They fully understand that concept. But they don't think that such a courtesy is their personal responsibility.

Being old seems to allow for a double standard wherein everyone else must be quiet so *you* can hear the performance, but that when *you* would rather talk than hear the performance or comment loudly on or about the performance, nobody else's inability to hear or enjoy factors into the courtesy equation.

That is why I found myself shushing the two old ladies sitting in front of me in the movies as they jabbered away about how the female lead in the production has aged over the last couple of years.

"Ladies, please be considerate," I pleaded. "I'm missing the dialog."

"Dialog, shmialog," one of them indignantly responded. "You're a young man and have good ears, so leave us alone."

"They're not good enough to hear over your conversation," I retorted. "Please don't make me call over the usher."

"You call the usher," the second old lady piped in, "and I'll tell him that you have been hitting on us!"

"Your deportment is disgraceful and shameful," I angrily responded.

"So sue us," the first lady replied.

This encounter forced me to find a pragmatic solution. I changed my seat to one a good twenty feet from where the old ladies were sitting.

"Oy! You stepped on my bunion!" shouted the elderly gentleman in the seat next to my relocation.

At this point, I arose from my seat, mumbled some well-directed expletive under my breath, and decided that I did not have to stay because I already had figured out the end of the picture.

The next morning, I took out a membership at my neighborhood video rental store and subscribed to Netflix. I really enjoy movies but have concluded that they are most enjoyable in the privacy of my own home where the only occasional noise distraction is the sound of my neighbor flushing his toilet or the frequent screeching siren of the rescue squad ambulance on its way to the hospital.

Subscribing to my cash is king philosophy, Netflix is much more economical than the $5.00 to $7.00 per Senior ticket price exacted by most of the local movie houses. My living room couch is infinitely more comfortable than the seat at most movie houses, my own popcorn does not cost me $6.00 a serving, and there are no old ladies present to disturb my enjoyment. Further, if I accidentally step on my own corn, I do not cry out!

CHAPTER SEVEN
A TRIP TO THE FARMERS' MARKET

Farmers' markets are a phenomenon that has sprung up in recent years in most urbanized areas around the United States. They do, however, differ in size, convenience of location, and the variety and pricing of products offered as compared to local supermarkets.

Price appears to be the leading factor that drives the underlying success of many farmers' markets, but the reference to price in this context applies only to the cost and quality of the merchandise and not to the price of the social costs one is obliged to pay for the privilege of getting at the produce and product bargains.

At most conventional supermarkets, the customer is afforded a nice, wide and fully paved parking stall, a sturdy and well maintained shopping cart and a courteous, concerned and non gum chewing cashier at the checkout who at least *pretends* that she gives a crap about your patronage.

And, the aisles are wide enough for two fat horses to pass each other, and the merchandise is artistically displayed to entice the customer to make as many impulse purchases as possible.

And well it should be so, considering that the 99 cents per pound tomatoes at the farmers' market cost $2.29 per pound at the supermarket!

My first encounter with a local farmers' market occurred on one of those rare Southeast Florida mornings when not a cloud appeared in the sky, the roads were not wet from intermittent showers, and the humidity was almost tolerable.

As I pulled into the parking lot I found myself stacked up behind two vehicles with handicap license plates that were unloading passengers in the driveway rather than doing same in a nearby parking stall.

When I finally spotted a vacant parking stall and the two vehicles in front of me had moved, I attempted to angle into the slot only to realize that one of the two contiguous autos, a humongous vintage Cadillac with New York license plates and obviously belonging to a snowbird, was parked 18 inches over the dividing line, thus making it impossible for any vehicle save a motorcycle or a Yugo to park in the space.

Undaunted, I decided to follow the lead of other rude and inconsiderate patrons and park my vehicle along the perimeter of the exit driveway. I duly noted the DO NOT PARK HERE signage along the driveway and implicitly acknowledged that the management would not tow cars for fear of losing customer patronage.

On my way to the entrance I could not help but notice two senior gentlemen each with their vehicles halfway into a vacant parking stall, yelling at each other about who got there first.

Once inside the shed-like building which housed this basically produce operation, I selected a shopping cart from among the World War II vintage relics which were offered by the management as a means of transporting purchases to a checkout. Most were rusted out with parts missing, but I found one that actually had all four wheels, no cigar butts or dirty tissues in the bottom, and no greasy or wet fingerprints on the handle.

I then dutifully went from display to display, dodging oncoming shopping carts, squeezing past old and obese patrons who were handling every fruit or vegetable in the display until finding the most desirable specimen, and finally reached the end of the ordeal with a head of crisp lettuce, two pounds of Pink Lady applies, and a hunk of $2.99 per pound aged cheddar cheese.

First, however, I had to dodge a number of loaded shopping carts which had been temporarily abandoned in the middle of narrow aisles while their users walked into other aisles to shop.

And, of course, I had given up being waited on at the fresh fish counter because a gaggle of old ladies pushed in ahead of me and rudely insisted, despite my protests, that they were waiting there long before I had arrived at the counter.

I am sure that one of these ladies was the same one I had observed at the cheese display inhaling most of the free samples and coughing on the ones she left for others.

As I gratefully had my merchandise checked out by an indifferent, gum chewing checker who obviously did not care whether I lived or died, I calculated that I had saved $3.92 over the pricing of similar merchandise at my local supermarket.

Finally, I ditched the shopping cart relic outside of the front door and made a beeline for my car. When I arrived at the car I saw a new and very large dent on the driver's side of the front fender. There was no note on the windshield identifying the culprit or leaving any insurance information.

I cannot help but believe that the senior perpetrator of this dastardly deed took great pains to teach his or her own children always to do the right thing. Perhaps sun and humidity in Florida have a meltdown effect on one's sense of integrity!

After I got over my anger, I submitted the claim to my automobile insurance carrier. My policy had a $500.00 deductible for collision. The repair cost $1154.25.

Future food shopping defaulted to my local supermarket. From an accountant's perspective, the numbers added up to a lower total despite the higher product prices!

CHAPTER EIGHT
THE RETIREMENT ADVISOR

Palm Beach County, Florida is certainly not an inexpensive place to live. If you are looking for an inexpensive place to live, you might try the Carolinas, Tennessee, or Vermont.

Most of the people who choose to retire to Palm Beach County have made their fortunes elsewhere and have planned ahead in order to be able to afford to come here in the first place. So, do they really need a new investment or retirement advisor?

That is why it is a mystery to me as to why investment advisors proliferate the landscape in these parts. They offer free luncheon, seminars and lots of up front gratis advice in their efforts to lure you into their advisory dens.

Once they hook you in, they exact between 1% and 2.5% annually on the average, of the total amount you have invested with them; and if you reinvest your profits, they charge that amount again on the incremental gain you have left in the account for reinvestment.

Many retirees who bring their assets to Florida have managed their own money previously, but the lure of being able to retire trouble free and problem free feeds into the hype of the investment advisors who assure you that they can do much better than you did on your own and more than justify what they take off the top.

Although everyone knows that the stock and bond markets are cyclical, many fail to realize that what the advisors take off the top in the way of fees is paid periodically to them whether or not they have made any money for you in a given payment cycle. Only a mathematical nincompoop would not understand that in cyclical markets, and with fees taken again on the profit increment, the actual fees taken are significantly higher than the stated percentages! (This assumes that they make a profit for you!)

My epiphany began one morning when I went to my mailbox and discovered no less than three such free meal with seminar invitations from three different retirement guru organizations. One was from a C.P.A. firm which proffered tax advice designed to minimize the Government's take on your profits. Another was from a law firm that offered to help redo your wills and trusts so as to conform to Florida law. The third was from an independent investment counseling firm which merely managed investments for a fee but otherwise did not directly handle money nor hold your equities in their account.

I was so intrigued by so many offers for freebies that I decided to employ a scientific method for determining which one I might consider to choose. The featured menu item on the C.P.A.'s solicitation was skirt steak with key lime pie for dessert. The law firm offered stuffed halibut with apple pie for dessert. The investment counselor's menu held out a choice between crab cakes and lamb chops with chocolate truffle for dessert.

My preference was definitely skirt steak and apple pie, so although I felt I would probably glean more useful information from the law firm's presentation, I opted for the C.P.A. menu.

After I had phoned in my reservation, my accountancy background compelled me to rethink the equation. After all, apple pie was a good treat, too. So I picked up the phone and called the reservation number for the law firm's presentation and secured myself a place at that seminar, too.

As I was about to discard the solicitation from the independent investment advisor, I remembered that I had not enjoyed a good lamb chop meal for some time, so I picked up the phone again and made a third reservation at that seminar.

The next day's mail delivery brought two more new solicitations from wealth advisors. I quickly perused their menus, totally ignoring the content of their respective lectures, realized that these seminars were given on days other than the ones for which I had already made reservations, and secured places at both of those lectures.

Now I could enjoy a freebie lunch every day of the next week and not be bored with any lack of variety in the food offerings. Actually, I was able to consume so much free food at these luncheons that it salved my prior decision not to patronize the restaurants offering price cut dinners to early bird diners.

And, the stream of free seminar luncheons have kept on coming so thick and fast that my food bill each and every week has been significantly and selectively reduced.

Although I usually take my MP3 player to these seminars and clandestinely enjoy classical music, I must confess that as an additional benefit I occasionally listen and have absorbed a handful of valuable gems about retirement from the sponsors of the luncheons. Consequently, I have no interest in or need to pay for any of the courses dealing with retirement which are offered by the local universities. This is a bonus which helps preserve my cash reserve.

In conclusion, it is now no wonder to me why the sponsoring gurus have to charge the kind of fees they exact for managing the investments of the few who sign on: when the pickings are slim, the profits must be fat!

CHAPTER NINE

WINNING THE LOTTERY AND
SIMILAR GAMES OF CHANCE

In Florida, it is illegal for vendors to sell lottery tickets to persons under 18 years of age. Maybe one day, a lame duck legislator with nothing to lose politically will introduce legislation prohibiting the sale of lottery tickets to persons *over* 65 years of age.

Frankly, I have been appalled by the number of seniors, many of them living on Social Security, who religiously stand in line twice a week and shell out untold dollars to purchase Florida's lottery tickets. Many of them sincerely believe that they will win someday, despite the fact that they stand a better chance of being struck by lightning or blown away by a tornado while standing in line to purchase their lottery tickets!

I have had to ask myself whether these people possess any more common sense than the persons under eighteen years of age who are legally prohibited from participating.

Further, I am astounded by the proliferation of gaming casinos frequented by the seniors who regularly go there, admitting before the fact that they are going to lose money and limiting themselves to pre-determined amounts of inevitable loss.

The logic of all this is contrary to my common sense thinking, probably because I am fairly astute when it comes to working with numbers and always focusing upon ways to conserve my cash.

With three million dollars in the bank from the sale of my accounting practice, perhaps I consider myself above the desperate crowd; but even with that degree of wealth available, I still would not purchase lottery tickets or frequent gambling casinos for fear of outliving my personal money supply. If you gamble and perchance win big once, you are hooked and begin to sow the seeds of your own financial destruction!

Many of my cohorts who consider going to a gambling casino to be a form of entertainment and a good time look upon me as a skinflint and a party pooper with an anal retentive personality problem. Screw them!

Nevertheless, although I stick to my principles, I occasionally defy my own logical thinking by purchasing lottery tickets, but only when the jackpot exceeds $15 Million Dollars, or by frequenting one of the casinos only when a Cadillac is being given away on any particular weekend.

Intellectually, I acknowledge that what I have chosen to do is really a contradiction in terms, but unlike columns of accounting numbers which are always supposed to add up to the same sum no matter how many times a given set of numbers is run on a calculator, illogic and luck can sometimes be productive bed partners: some lucky patrons occasionally win despite their stupidity about gambling odds!

When I capitulate to greed in this fashion, I do not stop to reason out that the larger the jackpot, the greater the volume of hysterical participation to win the elusive payoffs would be, thus reducing the probability of being the winner even further than with smaller jackpots.

Not everyone (including myself) who goes to the casino on Cadillac giveaway weekend is enamored of Cadillacs, but the immediate resale value of same greatly exceeds that of a new Toyota Corolla, which is the usual giveaway.

My compatriots at the country club are gambling freaks: they participate in pooled lottery purchases, football and basketball pools, and other gambling opportunities, but I refuse to participate in any kind of pool save for the one in the backyard of my current condo residence and in which I enjoy a daily dip. Odds are in my favor that it will keep me cool daily!

CHAPTER TEN
WARDING OFF THE CROC IN THE GAZOOBACKS

Now that I have retired, I have leisure time to think about all of my physical ills, both real and imagined. Things were actually not that different prior to my retirement, but now I can afford the luxury of paying more attention to the afflictions of the body.

Further, the emotional difficulties that manifested themselves after moving to Florida in a retirement mode compounded the overall feeling that all was not right with me, so I have concluded that I had better pay attention to the entire problem of maintaining good health.

As with most senior retirees in these parts, I have a medical insurance plan in which the primary coverage comes through Medicare with the insurance company affording wraparound coverage for the portion of medical services recognized by Medicare but paid by Medicare only to the tune of 80% of the Medicare allowed fee.

Very early on I discovered via several inquiries and visits to doctors' offices that the general response of the medical community to this Medicare driven affront is simply not to serve Medicare patients, or in the alternative, give them their money's worth in the form of cursory physicals and truncated bedside manner care.

Nevertheless, unless I opt to travel back to New York to have every physical ill attended to, I had to get with the program and either have my insurance bite the dust and pay full list price out of my own pocket or suffer the slings and arrows of the reduced level of care which the system has perpetrated.

I was further confronted with the new and growing option known as "the boutique doctor," a program wherein, for an annual upfront fee of between $1,500.00 to $10,000.00, a patient can guarantee unto himself immediate access to his favorite doctor offering this preferential plan.

This doctor would actually have the time to express genuine care and concern for his patients because he no longer had to worry about the paucity of the insurance reimbursements (which he got in addition to the boutique fees) or the beaurocratic delay involved in getting paid from the government and/or the insurance carrier.

I own up to being a skinflint and a scaredycat and feel that the medical profession has overstepped the bounds of propriety and has violated its Hippocratic oath by daring to discriminate in favor of patients with more money than the average retiree. Further, I fear I might run out of money prior to dying if I wasted it on such things like boutique physicians.

Anyhow, I firmly believe that the mind controls the wellness of the rest of the body, so I recently have begun to meditate daily after visiting the County Library and boning up on the various methodologies for such an undertaking.

As part of my meditation, I have developed my own mantra which I recite over and over every morning upon awakening. Here it is: "I don't give a crap about yesterday. That's history. I don't care about tomorrow.

Tomorrow may never come. I do give a crap about today because today is in the here and now and is the only true meaning. I do not have time to be sick because I must spend all of my energies enjoying the here and now. Enjoying the here and now is my mission for today."

And that is how I have come to grips with my own mortality and my retirement situation and have set out to fill my days with meaningful pastimes (such as meditating and sponging freebie seminar luncheons) designed to make me forget just how much I resent being retired and financially unproductive. Forsooth, it has been a particularly difficult feat for me not to give a crap about giving a crap (or convincing myself that I give a crap).

CHAPTER ELEVEN

HELP! HELP! MY RETIREMENT HOUSE IS UNDERWATER!

During the real estate value run ups of the Nineties, it was conventional wisdom to believe that home ownership was one of the most secure and promising routes to comfortable retirement.

Values climbed like clockwork, our equity in our homes escalated, home equity loan second mortgages were the vogue, and very little attention was paid to the historically cyclical nature of all investment markets.

If you are lucky enough to have paid off the mortgage on your principal residence and are contemplating retirement to warmer climes, you should not be thinking in terms of selling your present home and reinvesting the proceeds in a mortgage free retirement home.

The reason I say this is that your retirement home should not be treated like a potentially profitable real estate investment but rather as a place to live only. The realities of today's real estate market must be taken into consideration.

The current Federal tax laws permit most seniors with middle priced homes to sell them at a profit and avoid paying capital gains on the profit spread. It would seem to make more sense to repatriate those dollars into a different kind of investment which would provide an annual income to supplement Social Security income.

Very few of us foresaw the ongoing decline in real estate values, but I guess it was lucky for me when I decided (actually, I had no choice because I lost my marital home in my divorce) never to buy a retirement home but rather to rent in perpetuity.

If you have some kind of psychological difficulty coming to grips with this concept, consider that a leasehold also is actually a form of *ownership* for a finite period.

When you come right down to it, unless you know the formula for living forever, even a fee simple deed ownership of a property conveys little more than a lifetime estate in a property with the additional privilege of designating by Will or default who will succeed you in ownership after your death.

And, of course, if the World comes to an end, every form of real estate so called ownership will be rendered irrelevant!

So, relieve yourself of any worry that your retirement residence might go under water from a cause other than flooding and become a happier and wiser renter. Should you at some point decide to return to your previous environment, you have just saved yourself some of the major headaches associated with fee ownership of your retirement residence.

Rents are low because of the glut of vacant properties available for sale or rent, and in many cases, desperate landlords are willing to subsidize your occupancy as an alternative to losing their properties altogether. *So, rent!*

CHAPTER TWELVE

IS A PLOT FOR PLOTZING A NEFARIOUS PLOT OR MERELY A PLAT?

Probably nowhere more than in south Florida will you be inundated with offers from cemeteries and funeral parlors with so called bargain solicitations urging you to make preparations ahead of time for your final resting place.

In all probability, you may have purchased plots near your prior up North residence or simply failed to give any thought to a final resting place.

Consideration of this solemn undertaking, (excuse the pun), should be approached from a practical perspective if you are a senior of average means. Many of the offerors are willing to sign you up on an extended payment plan, but I have not yet seen a contract which cancels the balance of your payments should you happen to die prior to paying in full.

If the latter scenario comes to pass, the balance due would come out of your estate or would have to be paid by grieving relatives. The net result would be that your grieving beneficiaries would either be out the balance due or would inherit a smaller estate from you.

Knowing human nature, either scenario would leave them pissed, whether or not they would overtly own up to such feelings.

If you think *my* perspective on this dilemma is warped or jaundiced, I want you to consider how often *you* have visited graves of your dearly departed relatives no matter how close your relationship with the decedents may have been during their lifetimes.

It should be obvious to you, now, that even if you refuse to admit it, the people in the cemetery are deceased, and when you visit their graves, should you ever even do so, you are doing so for *yourself only!*

Cemeteries are for the *living!* The deceased do not know the difference. Therefore, why on earth should you endure any costly payout or up front egregious lump sum payment just so your surviving relations can enjoy an expensive place *not to visit!*

If they are so intent upon visiting with themselves at your gravesite after you are dead, let *them* pay for the privilege!

A growing solution to this conundrum is the thinking green alternative known as cremation. It is a hot topic among seniors! (Pardon the pun). It is inexpensive, and if you acknowledge your willingness to be cremated by written instructions prior to death, the small payment for same up front should not kill you, *(again* excuse the pun), or make your responsible survivors too upset should they have to foot the bill in your stead for this service.

CHAPTER THIRTEEN
FINAL CONCLUSIONS

Almost two years have now elapsed since I made my almost mindless decision to abjure the realm of the familiar in New York and relocate myself summarily to the subtropical paradise of Palm Beach County Florida.

The time has now come for an honest assessment of my situation in terms of the here and now and what may be in store for the future (if there is one).

I am still divorced from my wife, and I still do not know exactly why she left me. By now, I care even less to know why that happened than I did *when* it happened.

My two sons of that marriage still continue to have little to do with me, the only significant difference being that they have little to do with me in Florida rather than having little to do with me in New York.

I do not miss any of my old "friends" from New York because they never really were my friends. One of my former tennis regulars came to Boca Raton a few months ago for a brief vacation. I bumped into him strictly by accident in a restaurant, and it was obvious from his demeanor that he could not wait until I excused myself from the chance meeting.

As far as making new friends is concerned, I have found the climate in my country club difficult to decipher. Most country club members are not spring chickens. They come here with all of their old baggage from their former lives and, for the most part, do not plan to live long enough to make new "lifelong" friendships. They are polite and cordial but the scene can be an isolated one, especially for a divorcee or widow or widower.

I have gone to some of the singles mingles both at my own country club and affairs jointly sponsored between the clubs. Possibly, I have become too critical and too cautious in my old age, but one of greatest fears is that some chance female I might meet at one of these events will "Google" me on the internet and somehow discover that I am a man of means and come after me for my assets only.

Possibly, this would be no different had I remained in New York, but the vulnerability factor is greatly magnified once you have transplanted yourself into a new territory with which you have far less familiarity than where you originally lived for a long time and had deep roots.

My cousins and other relatives still live in the Northeast. Our family cemetery has not relocated to Florida from Long Island. Many days I feel that I made a mistake transplanting myself so far away from what used to be so familiar.

I think it might take many years to adapt to my new environment, if ever at all. That is why I think like a pragmatist. I still rent my residence rather than own it, because if I decide to go back to New York I will not be saddled with the problem of disposing of a home in a very downtrodden real estate market.

I know that I am not alone in my thinking. A significant portion of the New Jersey shore began to be inhabited since the early 1060s, in Active Adult communities, by New Yorkers and New Jersey residents who migrated in retirement to Florida and other far away warm climates but who moved back because they missed their families, lifelong friends, and local institutions and affiliations.

In conclusion, the best advice I can proffer is that you keep an open mind after you have transitioned, and never be afraid to admit to yourself that the choice you made might not have been the correct one or might possibly have now outlived its usefulness.

But do not be too quick to reverse your steps until you think long and hard as to what kind of lifestyle might possibly await you should you return to your former and more familiar environment. Things may have changed in your absence. Most importantly, do not forget that you gave away your woolen underwear and your snow shovel!

*   *   *

"READER HOMEWORK WORKSHEET SECTION"

Dear Reader:

In all probability you purchased this little volume because you hoped to gain some insight into the likely pitfalls inherent in a decision to migrate at retirement to a new environment.

The author hopes that the experiences of Sheldon Brodsky (not his real identity) have given you a small window of insight into why unplanned migration may result in negative consequences.

The purpose of these blank worksheet papers is to afford you an opportunity to do some pre-migration research, memorialize your concerns, and write down precisely how you plan to meet each of the challenges. Be specific.

Notice that the author has supplied a generous number of pages upon which you should do your pre-migration homework. He has done this because he is of the opinion that your task at hand is monumental if you want the end result to fall within the parameters of your expectations.

GOOD LUCK!"